Blanchardstown, Castleknock and the Park

'twixt Liffey and Tolka

Paintings by Dónal MacPolin
Text by Peter Sobolewski

Cottage
Publications

First published by Cottage Publications,
Donaghadee, N. Ireland 2001.
Copyrights Reserved.
© Illustrations by Dónal Mac Polin 2001.
© Text by Peter Sobolewski 2001.
All rights reserved.
No part of this book may be reproduced or
stored on any media without the express
written permission of the publishers.
Design & origination in Northern Ireland.
Printed & bound in Singapore.

ISBN 1 900935 22 8

The Author

Peter Sobolewski is a graduate of University College Galway and completed his post-graduate studies at the London School of Economics. His interests are 20th Century International History and Local History.

Peter was born in Syracuse, New York, and raised in Kiltimagh, Co Mayo. He is a teacher at Coolmine Community School, Clonsilla, having previously taught in London, South Carolina and Drogheda.

He is the Author of the school series, *'Let's Look At History'*. His local history publications are *'The Blanchardstown Chronicle'* and *'Kiltimagh: Our Life and Times'*.

Peter lives in Dublin with his wife Muriel, and their three children Rory, Conor and Ciara.

The Artist

Dónal Mac Polin was born in Dublin but brought up in Moville, Co Donegal. He emigrated to England in 1963 and graduated in Art and Ceramics from Birmingham University. Returning to Ireland he has taught art at Coolmine Community School since 1975 and now lives in Blanchardstown.

He has exhibited paintings of Dublin and produced two limited editions of prints of his work.

Although a teacher of art, his main interest lies in traditional Irish boats. He has recently published a second edition to his 1990 book, *'The Drontheim, Forgotten Sailing Boat of the North Irish Coast'*.

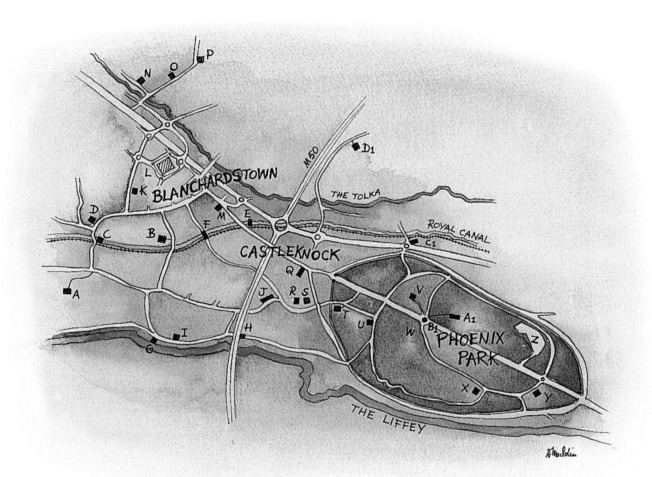

Contents

Beginnings

"Nothing happened for one hundred years and then everything changed overnight"

So said Shay Cullen a resident of Clonsilla, one of the villages that now makes up the Greater Blanchardstown Area. He is correct in his assessment. In a period of thirty years (1970-2000) the landscape has changed dramatically from rural to urban settlement.

By the 1960s Dublin was beginning to flourish as the country's economic, social and political capital – and the rise in population was reflected in this development. In 1841 the population of Dublin was 370,000. This rose to 795,000 in 1966 and the projection was 1.2 million by 1980. The government recognised the need for planning if the situation was to be controlled. It passed the wide-ranging Local Government (Planning and Development) Act in 1963, requiring each urban authority in Ireland to submit a development plan, within three years, to cover four specific areas:

- Land-use zoning for residential, commercial, industrial and other purposes
- Improvement of road and traffic conditions
- The renewal and development of obsolete areas
- The preservation, improvement and extension of amenities

As a result of this Act the Wright Report was published for the Dublin region in 1968. It proposed the development of three major growth centres in West Dublin - Tallaght, Clondalkin/Lucan and Blanchardstown. Each of these 'new towns' was to be a self-contained unit providing housing, services, jobs and amenities for their inhabitants. In the case of Blanchardstown this would be 100,000 persons.

So began the new Blanchardstown, yet the story of the Greater Blanchardstown Area really began about 350 million years ago, south of the equator and

Beginnings

under the sea in what geologists call the Carboniferous period.

A shallow clean warm sea covered much of what is now the central plain of Ireland. There was abundant life in the warm waters of this sea, especially shellfish and corals. These creatures extracted chemicals from the seawater to make their shells. When they died the shells accumulated on the sea bed. As time went on further layers were deposited and the lower layers were compressed into solid rock. This rock is limestone. Sometimes mud got mixed in these marine deposits and the resulting limestone has a dark earthy colour. Sometimes layers of mud were compressed between layers of limestone and these are known as shale.

Limestone is the main rock underlying West Dublin and is gently folded in a north-east to south-west direction. Much of the Greater Blanchardstown area is on the crest of such a fold and gives the appearance of being a plateau. Evidence of this limestone can be seen in the many quarries and rock outcrops in the area. Quarries near Scribblestown House, Ashtown and Hillbrook show strata of black earthy limestone and black shales. In all these places fossils, especially Trilobites were found. A little south of Castleknock, pale grey compact limestone can be seen in the quarries. The fossils found here include Productus, Spirifer, Euomphalus and Orthoceras.

While these carboniferous rocks were being formed, earth-shattering and land-forming geographical events were taking place. 'Ireland' was part of a landmass known as Laurasia which was drifting in a northerly direction. This journey took 'Ireland' 400 million years to reach its present-day position. And the weather was very different - the Ice Age was in progress.

The Ice Age began about 2 million years ago and ended about 10,000 years ago. There were many glacial periods during that time but the last one, known as the Midlandian, gave us the features we see today on the Irish landscape. During the Midlandian period, ice covered the central lowlands to a depth of 300 metres. In time there was a significant rise in temperature and the ice began to melt, covering the limestone with deposits of boulder clay. These deposits vary in depth. In parts of the Phoenix Park they barely cover the rock, while in the Castleknock area they are some 15 metres deep. The soils in West Dublin which have developed from this boulder clay are known as grey-brown podzolics. These are good all-purpose agricultural soils, and are particularly suited to pastoral farming.

A most interesting feature of glacial deposition found in this area is the esker. An esker is a long narrow ridge of sand and gravel winding its way across the landscape. It is thought eskers were formed by streams depositing sand and gravel as they flowed through glaciers, often to a height of 30 metres. The eskers in Dublin form part of the *Esker Riada* – the esker joining Dublin to Galway. In Celtic times the *Esker Riada* marked the dividing line between the northern kingdom of Conn of the Hundred Battles and the southern one of Mugha from whom Munster gets its name. Celtic man found another use for eskers – as routeways. The main road from the west to Dublin, the *Slighe Mór* ran along the *Esker Riada.* Another main routeway, the *Slighe Chualaun,* went from Tara through Blanchardstown into Dublin and on to Wicklow. Tara was the Seat of the High King of Ireland.

The Tolka and Liffey, the rivers which flow through this area, have links with this glacial period. While the Tolka is a post-glacial river it is thought that the water in the western part of its basin in pre-glacial times flowed into the Liffey, west of the Chapelizod gorge. The old river channel is now hidden beneath glacial deposits. The Liffey itself is a pre-glacial river, and its channel too was covered in glacial deposits. After the Ice Age it followed its old channel until it neared Chapelizod where it cut a short deep gorge through the carboniferous limestone, thereby forming a new channel.

As the glaciers retreated, vegetation appeared on the landscape. The initial tundra vegetation was moss, lichens and dwarf willow. In time the temperature rose, allowing birch, aspen and hazel to grow and spread, and man made his first appearance in this area.

The castle and grounds of Luttrellstown are among the most beautiful of the great homes of Ireland today. The estate's scenery is idyllic, yet in 1922 M.J.Burke wrote in the Saturday Herald:

"There is no more beautiful castle demesne in all county Dublin than that of Luttrellstown. There is no family whose name is associated with such bitter memories in the history of Ireland as are joined with the name of the "Luttrells". There is no spot in Ireland the mention of whose name conveyed more haunting fears to our fore fathers".

This was borne out when Henry White, ancestor of Lord Annaly, changed the estate's name to Woodlands.

Geoffrey Luttrell came to Ireland in 1204, and was granted the estate by King John as reward for loyal service. For the next four hundred years the Luttrells prospered, enjoying great wealth and distinction. Then the outbreak of the Jacobite War (1688) saw the beginning of the decline of their good name. At the time of Simon Luttrell, first Earl of Carhampton, 'Junius' wrote to the Duke of Grafton:

"There is a certain family in this country, on which nature seems to have entailed a hereditary baseness of disposition. As far as their history is known, the son has regularly improved upon the vices of his father, and has

taken care to transmit them pure and undiminished into the bosom of his successor".

By the 1790s agrarian and political unrest was rampant. As Commander of the British forces in Ireland, Henry Lawes Luttrell helped to pacify the country, ruthlessly quelling opposition, real or imagined. He became such a tyrant, especially in West Dublin, that two of his own workers planned to assassinate him. Pat Carthy and James Dunn lived outside the walls of Luttrellstown. The resources to carry this out were not forthcoming so they called their plan off. However, they were betrayed and arrested. While awaiting trial in prison they were tortured. They were convicted of treason, and on November 11, 1797, they were hanged, drawn and quartered in Jervis Street, Dublin.

Luttrellstown was sold to Mr Luke White in 1800. Today it is a luxury hotel.

Luttrellstown Castle

The old national school in Clonsilla can only be described as different when compared with the average national school built in rural Ireland in the nineteenth century. It is a tall, narrow, Dickensian looking building, the brainchild of whom is not recorded. Local gossip relates that the parish priest asked the owners of Luttrellstown Castle for a site on which to build the school. They refused and it is said that he retorted: *"I will build a school in spite of you and it will be visible no matter where you go* (on your estate)".

The reality was different and more complex. There was no national school in Clonsilla before 1854, so the local children attended Porterstown School. In 1852 Fr Dungan, the parish priest, learned to his horror that the Church of Ireland curate, the Rev Cooke, was using 'literature offensive to Catholic children' in Porterstown school. He would not tolerate proselytizing and all Catholic children were withdrawn from the school within a very short time. This action necessitated a new school and Fr Dungan turned his attention to providing it. He bought five acres of land from the Royal Canal Company and in less than two years the school was ready. The entry in Fr Dungan's diary for Jan 16, 1854 simply states:

"Opened new school at Clonsilla – 58 boys and 66 girls attended. Teachers – Timothy Looney and Mrs James Power".

The teachers lived in the apartments in the basement.

Funding for the school was always a problem and shortly before he died in 1868, Fr Dungan raffled his £12 watch. He did it by advertising in the Freeman's Journal. The raffle raised almost £95.

Clonsilla National School served the parish for nearly 110 years.

Clonsilla National School

The small, erstwhile rural, railway station at Clonsilla has never made pretentious claims of importance, yet its history has not been uneventful.

In Easter week 1916, 14 volunteers from Maynooth, led by Domhnall Ua Buachalla, walked along the banks of the Royal Canal to join in the rising in Dublin. When they reached Clonsilla Station they headed towards the Tolka, and from there to Parliament Street to deal with snipers at City Hall. Each man was armed with a single-barrelled shotgun and 24 cartridges! Meanwhile, an 18-pound battery from Athlone army barracks was being detrained at Blanchardstown by the British army. It was used to destroy barricades on Cabra Road and North Circular Road.

The station itself became a casualty during the Civil War when the signal box was blown up by Republicans.

Horses and cattle played a central role in the economy of the station. During World War I workhorses arrived at Clonsilla Station from all parts of Ireland for sale to the British Army. Local men then earned one sovereign taking 3 horses to the quays at the North Wall.

In his novel *Ulysses*, James Joyce mentions the commotion caused on the streets of Dublin by a drover herding his cattle to the market at Prussia Street. Clonsilla Station was the starting point for many of these herds. In retrospect one cannot help wondering what Joyce meant when he wrote:

"Wonder if that dodge works now getting dicky meat off the train at Clonsilla".

The gates were operated manually until recently when the station was updated to cater for the new commuter trains. Its very fine Victorian cast-iron railway bridge has thankfully been preserved.

Clonsilla Station

CLONSILLA

The serenity of St Mary's Church, Clonsilla, is a reminder of quieter rustic days in the not too distant past. Looking at the church from the east it conjures a picture of village tranquillity protected by its soothing treeline. Yet, like all pictures it has its shortcomings, for this holy place has had its peace shattered on many occasions.

The site of St Mary's has a long ecclesiastical history, dating back to the sixth century. St Mochta, the last surviving disciple of St Patrick, built his 'White Chapel' at nearby Coolmine, and Clonsilla became a cell or sept of the Coolmine Church. In the early part of the 13th century, the Benedictines were invited to the area by Sir John Luttrell. They accepted the invitation and built a Priory on the site of the old Celtic Church at Clonsilla. The Priory, now known as St Brigids, was dependent on the Benedictine house at Little Malvern, Worcestershire. The Luttrells had been given their land by King John and the local people often attacked the Priory, as in the 1360s, in an attempt to win their lands back. When the 1798 rebellion failed, the Church experienced its most goulish act – the grave of Colonel Henry Luttrell was burst open and his skull was smashed with a pickaxe.

The present church was built during the office of Archbishop Whately (1831-63). It is a fine rectangular building made of granite, with a pleasant looking tower at the west end.

One of its stained-glass windows is a vibrant depiction of a scene from the life of St Fiacra by Evie Hone (1894 - 1955). Fiacra is the patron saint of gardeners. In the past many of the Church's members worked as gardeners in the local large estates. Her work in glass was influenced by the great French artist, George Rouault and by Picasso.

St Mary's made headlines in the national press in July 1907, shortly after the robbery of the crown jewels from Dublin Castle. There were no leads in the investigation so a clairvoyant was engaged to help in the recovery of the jewels. While in a trance a voice said the missing jewels were hidden in Clonsilla Churchyard. The citizens of Dublin needed little encouragement, and, armed with shovels, descended in droves on St Mary's. They were not successful.

St Mary's Church
Clonsilla

In June 1990 the Royal Canal Amenity Group organised a week long boat rally along the Royal Canal. This was no ordinary rally – it was to celebrate the restoration of the canal, between Blanchardstown and Mullingar, to navigation. The canal had ceased to be a working canal in 1951, and over the next 40 years it was allowed to fall into a sad state of neglect.

The decision to build the Royal Canal was of dubious wisdom. The man behind the venture was John Binns, a wealthy shoemaker who was also a director and member of the Managing Committee of the Grand Canal Company. It seems that on many occasions he took decisions without consulting the other members. Eventually the members banded together to outvote him. Binns resigned after an acrimonious meeting, vowing to have his revenge by starting a rival company.

Work started on the Royal Canal in 1790, and almost immediately problems arose. No comprehensive survey had been carried out, so the estimated cost, £197,098, was meaningless. Even the costs of building were underpriced. To cut costs an engineer to oversee the work was not initially appointed, with dire consequences. The final cost was £1.5 million.

One of the major obstacles encountered in the construction of the canal was the hard band of black calcareous rock at Carpenterstown Quarry. It had originally estimated that the 2-mile stretch would cost £10,224 to quarry. The work was so difficult that the quarrymens' wages were doubled – from 1s 6d to 3s 4d per cubic yard – and the final cost was £41,969.

Although the canal company began its trade and passenger service in 1796 between Kilcock and Dublin, it was not until 1799 that boats stopped at Clonsilla. The fare from Clonsilla to Dublin, a distance of 6 miles, was 1s 7$\frac{1}{2}$d first class and 1s 1d second class.

Safety for the canal traveller could not be guaranteed. In the early 1800s attacks on canal boats caused serious disruption to trade. Ribbonmen (members of a rural protest movement) were mainly responsible, often beating the crew and destroying boats.

The most serious accident on the canal occurred on November 26, 1845, when the night boat to Longford crashed into the bank between Porterstown Bridge and Clonsilla Bridge. The evening was cold, wet and dark so the reluctant steersman gladly entrusted this task of steering to a free passenger, Patrick Teeling, in lieu of payment. Teeling was under the influence of drink and incapable of navigating the bend. Seventeen people, including children, lost their lives.

The Royal Canal

Alexander Kirkpatrick (1749-1818), after whom this bridge on the Royal Canal was named, was a member of a wealthy wool merchant family. Like many members of his class he sought social advancement and this was achieved by buying a country estate. Kirkpatrick bought Coolmine and for the next 30 years he played an active part in the economic and civic life of Blanchardstown, Dublin and Ireland.

The Kirpatricks who originally came from Scotland were very well connected. A daughter of the Scottish line married Count de Montijo and her daughter became the Empress Eugenie of Austria.

From 1773 the Kirpatricks lived at Drumcondra House (now All Hallows College) until they bought Coolmine from Robert Bolton (after whom Bolton Street is named) in 1782. Alexander first came to local prominence in 1792 when he became chairman of the Association for the Protections of Private Property in the United Districts of Castleknock, Leixlip, Chapelizod and Dunboyne. This was a time of serious social and political unrest in Ireland where law and order were breaking down. Local disturbances were discussed at the initial meeting, many complaining of the 'barbarous practice of killing sheep for the purpose of stealing their fat only'.

The early 1790s was a busy time for Kirkpatrick. He actively supported John Binns when the idea of the Royal Canal was mooted and became a shareholder in that project. In 1793 he first became a Director on the Board of the Bank of Ireland and served as Governor during the period 1812-14.

Even though the political situation was unstable, landowners in the Castleknock Union formed a Farmers Society in 1797. Its chairman was the Secretary of State, the Rt Hon Pelham and Alexander Kirkpatrick was treasurer. The foremost aim of the Society was to improve agriculture in the area. But it also wanted to motivate and reward 'faithful, industrious and sober servants and labourers'. It did so by offering a reward of £2 5s 6d to the 'labourer who shall appear to have brought up the greatest number of legitimate children in habits of industry to the age of 12 years'. By 1803 the Society felt it was time to go farther and discussed a scheme 'to encourage the industrious poor … during the summer months when they can earn most to lay up something against the time of need'. Members of the Society 'engaged to add as a gift a quarter of whatever sum any such poor person shall lay up', hopefully in the process cutting down the 'inclination to spend another sixpence idly at the alehouse'.

Kirkpatrick Bridge

Everybody living around here knows that the original mill was built overnight, but there is some disagreement about the exact circumstances.

It seems that one of the Luttrells, nobody seems to remember which one, was a spendthrift who was constantly short of money. So he did a deal with the devil. Luttrell would sell his soul to him in exchange for a substantial sum of money. The devil agreed, a date was set, the deal was struck, and Luttrell proceeded to a life of pleasure.

Seven years to the day the devil came to claim his due. He appreciated Luttrell's gaming nature and felt he should give him a sporting chance to redeem his soul. A local child wrote this sequel in 1936:

"The devil told Lord Luttrell to give him three things to do, and if he could fool him in any of them he would be let off. But if he did not succeed the devil would bring him down to hell. Lord Luttrell told him to build him a flourmill in the night. The next morning his Lordship took a walk around his ground. When he came to a part that looks down on the Liffey he saw the completed mill. His Lordship had failed."

Luttrell knew that if he did not succeed in the next attempt he would not succeed in the third.

"So he told the devil to make him a rope out of the sand down by the Liffey. The devil gathered the sand and began his task. But the sand was breaking all the time. The devil asked if he could put manure through the sand, Luttrell said 'No, you must make it out of the sand only'. The devil failed and Lord Luttrell got off free".

The mill is now owned by Fingal County Council, and there are plans to restore it to working order again as a public resource.

The Devil's Mill

"Where the Strawberry Beds sweep down to the Liffey,
You'll kiss away the worries from my brow,
I love you well today, and I'll love you more tomorrow,
If you've ever loved me Molly love me now."

(The Ferryman)

The northern bank of the river Liffey, starting at Knockmaroon Hill and going towards Lucan, has been described as one of Co Dublin's 'scenic gems'. Known to Dubliners as the Strawberry Beds, this delightful valley has been called by Arthur Young, the 18th century English agricultural commentator, *"the most beautiful environ in Dublin"*. For the antiquarian Weston Joyce its appeal is the *"picturesque sylvian scenery"*. The valley slopes are steep and take full advantage of their south facing aspect and are *"particularly well adapted to the culture of strawberries and industry identified with this place from time immemorial"*.

In the 19th century 'The Beds' was a popular resort for working class Dubliners. Their lives in the city have invariably been described as dreary, but once they got to 'The Beds' *"the sounds of revelry filled the air"*, banishing dreariness for a time.

The strawberry season began in June, so on Sunday afternoons jaunting cars plied between Carlisle (O'Connell) Bridge and 'The Beds' ferrying day-trippers at 3d a seat. On arrival, strawberries could be purchased from vendors, served on a cabbage leaf at a cost of 2d per leaf. Once the strawberries were consumed, energising walks along the riverbank could follow, just the right ingredient to prepare the visitor to appreciate the festive music of the fiddler and piper emanating from one of the many pubs and shebeens in the locality.

Strawberry Beds

Writing in the Daily Telegraph in 1985 Jeremy Lewis bemoaned the disappearance of genuine old pubs in England. *"My own notion of Paradise Lost"*, he writes, beckons from the other side of the Irish Sea. He was writing of the Wren's Nest in the Strawberry Beds, and well he might, as this is no ordinary pub. This is a small, cosy pub nestling into the steep side of the Liffey Valley, and it does not open until 9pm!

The Wren's Nest goes back a long way – to 1588! There is a worn beam inside on which this date has been carved. Originally it was a coach house. *"Its really like a club"*, says Una O'Rourke, *"catering for its regulars who come from as far away as Howth and Wicklow"*. The warm atmosphere has been created by the Ennis/O'Rourke proprietorship which stretches back to the early 1800s.

One of these proprietors was certainly unique. Hughie Ennis was an opera buff who seemed more interested in creating a cultural environment than enriching himself as an innkeeper. He loved nothing better than discussing the arias of Caruso or John McCormack. During the war years Hughie travelled to St Jame's Gate by donkey and cart to collect kegs of stout, and all who frequented the Wren's Nest were entertained by his melodious renditions as he bottled the black stuff.

"Do you know who that is?" a regular asked his wife when two visitors left the Wren's Nest one night. *"His face is certainly familiar"* she replied, *"does he come from Blanchardstown?"* The visitor was the rock star Mick Jagger. The pub has certainly had its share of celebrities. The Dubliners played there on many an occasion, as did Seamus Ennis, the Uillean Piper. The writer Brendan Behan caused Hughie to frown more than a few times. No such thing happened with the visits of actors Siobhan McKenna and members of RTE's rural soap, 'The Riordans'. More recently the pub played host to Julia Roberts and Daniel Day Lewis.

Thankfully the future of this unique pub is in safe hands.

The Wren's Nest

It is said that the eight cottages on the Sandpit Road, know as the Sandpit Cottages, got their name from the quarry behind them. There are a few quarries in the area, and it was from one of these that the sand was acquired to build Collin's Army Barracks. The cottages were built by the Guinness family for their workers in the 1890s, yet not all who lived there worked for the Guinnesses.

Until recent developments in the area, life for those who lived in the cottages was quiet and countrylike. Well, for most of the time. Cattle being unloaded at Clonsilla Station on their way to Prussia Street Market were always a topic of discussion. This was not just a noisy journey for the inhabitants of the sandpits. As there were no gates blocking off the entrance to the lane at the back of the cottages people recall bewildered cattle darting into the lane and causing mayhem – at 2 o'clock in the morning!

A more vibrant topic of discussion was the events of a Sunday morning in the early 1940s. Mrs Mary Traynor takes up the story. *"We had just come home from mass when we heard the droning noise of German planes overhead. Next moment we heard machinegun fire, the bullets ripping into the ground just a few yards up from the cottages. Afterwards we were told that the Germans were using up their ammunition to lighten their planes. This would save fuel for the return journey".*

The district always had its characters. "You With the Hat" caused great merriment for the children. And many remember "Holy Ginger". On one occasion he was visiting John Fagan, the local tailor. John had been ironing, and unknown to his visitor the 'goose-iron' (a horseshoe for resting the iron) was very hot. The visitor picked it up and instead of instantly dropping it he passed it from one hand to the other shouting *"Holy Ginger, Holy Ginger"*.

John himself was no ordinary tailor. His clients not only came from Ireland, but from as far as Britain and America, such was his fame for making hunting clothes. The gentry came from all over Dublin and Meath for the hunts, and John bedecked many of them in their red coats and jodhpurs and he made a good living from his work – when they paid him!

In recent times another craftsman 'par excellence' came from this district too, Cathal Gannon. Restoring antiques was his speciality, but making harpsichords was his great love.

The Sandpit Cottages

Anybody who travels from the Clonsilla Roundabout to the Blanchardstown by-pass cannot fail to notice the 'ringfort' at Coolmine surrounded by four imposing trees. Its juxtaposition with the gleaming new Town Centre reminds one that this area has been inhabited for a long time.

Ringforts, or raths, were farmsteads and come from pre-Norman times. The ringfort at Coolmine is slightly oval in shape and measures 50 x 30 metres. But it is different from other ringforts as it is said to be the site of St Mochta's Church. Mochta, who died in August 534 was 'the last of St Patrick's missionary saints'. Tradition says he was a gentle and humble man, with a wonderful sense of humour.

The story is told that during one of his journeys, Mochta and his monks camped in the open for the night. As they slept robbers came and stole their horses. The robbers travelled all night on the horses but when morning came they had made no progress. They knew a superior power was at work and they wanted to return the horses. When they tried to dismount they were unable to do so. When Mochta realised what had happened he said to his monks, *"Go to that place where your horses have been tired with vain labour and release those wretches who still remain on their backs"*. The robbers, we are told, repented gladly.

Today nothing remains of Mochta's Church. However, in 1850, while the field was being ploughed, a considerable number of human bones were turned up by the plough. The land was owned by Alexander Kirkpatrick and he had them collected and buried. He then paid a local tradesman named Mangan to erect a memorial on the burial place. The memorial consisted of a cylindrical pillar of cement with a domed top surmounted by a wooden cross. On one side of the pillar was the inscription 'To the Unknown Dead'. This find of bones suggests a forgotten cemetery, and the cemetery would have been in close association with the site of the church.

Coolmine "Ringfort" – St Mochtas

When the Wright Report recommended the building of three satellite towns around Dublin in 1968, each catering for a population of 100,000, Dublin County Council responded to meet changing circumstances. It adopted a development plan (1972) which provided for new town centres. As a result, under Green Property Management, Blanchardstown Centre opened its doors on October 16, 1996.

Architecturally, the Centre is designed to be customer friendly. The design of the central area, the main complex, is based on graceful semi-circular arches, encasing two acres of glass. Each of the four entrances is designed as a spacious pavilion, with high superstructures built in brilliant white steel, and with bright coloured sails, like those of a great ship. This airy spaciousness with its natural light dispels any sense of crowding.

While the centre is primarily there to provide a comprehensive range of shops and services – 30 million shoppers visited the centre in its first two years – it has a definite social function. It encourages local community groups to use its central area for cultural activities, an offer taken up by nearby Coolmine Community School for concerts and fashion shows. To date the 'piece de resistance' was that school's production of Shaun Davey's 'The Pilgrim'. An audience of 1,200 heard actor Ben Kingsley, famous for his film role as Gandhi, narrate the performance. The Irish Times wrote (March 21, 2000):

"It is rare for major cultural events to take place in suburban shopping centres, but tonight the retailers of Blanchardstown will disprove the rule with an exception that is truly breath-taking in its audacity"

The next day that paper said:

"this was a splendidly executed performance".

The planners wanted the centre to be a socially vibrant area, and this necessitated other activities on its 90-acre site. It encompasses apartments, an Arts Centre with the *'Draiocht'* theatre, Blanchardstown Library, a Medical Centre, County Council offices, an Oratory, Cinemas and Leisure facilities.

Blanchardstown Centre

Driving on the Blanchardstown by-pass towards Navan the observant traveller can be pleasantly surprised by the unexpected image of St Brigid's Church spire. It seems so out of place in Ireland, more fitting perhaps to a village in France.

The foundation stone for this church was laid by Fr Joseph Joy Dean on October 13, 1835. Fr Dean was a colourful character hailing from the Black Mountain, Hannastown, Co Antrim. He was born about 1752 and was educated for the priesthood at the Irish College, Salamanca, Spain where he was ordained in 1792. He is thought to have spent some time in Rome before returning to Ireland. No doubt his travels on the continent influenced his aesthetic development, hence the spire which is said to be of Flemish design.

The Ireland he returned to was in the throes of rebellion and soon he would hear of the execution of his first cousin Henry Joy McCracken, a leader of the United Irishmen, for his role in the 1798 rebellion. Both were grandsons of Francis Joy, founder of the News Letter.

The Blanchardstown to which Fr Dean was posted was a small hamlet where many of his parishioners worked as agricultural labourers on local estates. Yet over the next thirty years they would generously contribute, from their limited resources, to the cost of the church.

One notices that St Brigid's is built on a side road off the Main Street – a relic from Penal Days when mass houses were not to be conspicuous. In 1838 John D'Alton described the new church as a *"commodious chapel, 90 feet in length by 35 in breadth and 33 in height, admirably, yet simply ventilated"*. Fr Dean died in 1836 so he never saw his completed church. The church, in fact, was only a shell of a building at that date. Work commenced on the gallery and ceiling in 1856. The spire was completed two years later and in 1862 the bell was installed.

St Brigid's Church, Blanchardstown

By the mid 1980s Parslickstown House had fallen into a seriously derelict state and faced demolition. Fortunately the house came into the ownership of Fingal County Council, was restored, and is now used by the Greater Blanchardstown Development Project. All sorts of groups use it, from small businesses to welfare rights groups to adult education groups.

The Carr Family were the original owners of Parslickstown House (built around 1840), with its 164-acre farm. According to local folklore the money to purchase this property came from a most unorthodox source. There was a man being executed in England. Before he was executed he was asked if he had anything to say. He asked if there was anybody there from Mulhuddart. There was, and he told him that if he went back to Blair's wall he would find a pot of gold. So the man returned to Blanchardstown and proceeded to dig. He found the gold and it was with this money Parslickstown was purchased.

Francis Carr was an ardent supporter of the Land League in the 1880s. During the Land War a grand Land League rally was held on the front lawn of Parslickstown House. Charles Stuart Parnell attended and later had lunch at the house. He almost did not get to eat his lunch however because, according to tradition, one of the family dogs crept in through an open window and was caught just seconds away from devouring it.

"Daring Rescue by Herd", was the dramatic headline on the Saturday Post. It referred to the rescue of young William Carr from drowning, but the reality was not quite so startling. While playing at the Tolka, William fell into the river and was pulled out by a cowman named Christy Chrichly. A reporter from the Post heard the story while visiting 'The Shanty' public house. The punchline was rather lost when he reported that the water level of the Tolka was seven inches.

Parslickstown House

Just down the road from Mulhuddart Church stands the rather unique shrine known as Lady's Well. Cheerfully painted in white and blue the little church-like shrine (in dimensions approx. 5ft high, 5ft 6 inches wide and 9ft long) is said to have been built in the 18th century. The shrine covers a holy well which was dedicated to the Virgin Mary in Anglo-Norman times.

From time immemorial water has been regarded as a potent symbol of the sacred. The Druids in Celtic Ireland worshipped wells and they divined the future by gazing into them. Even more so, water has a central role in Christianity, so when the Celts were converted their holy wells were subsumed into the life of the Christian Church. In this way Lady's Well became a place of pilgrimage for the citizens of Dublin.

Writing in the 'Journey to Lough Derg' in 1740, Isaac Butler described devotions at Lady's Well:

"About midway ascending to the church is an excellent well. It is carefully walled in, and several large trees about it. Here on the 8th September, a great pattern is kept with a vast concourse of all sexes and ages for many miles, upwards of 80 tents being pitched here, furnished with all kinds of liquors and provisions for the refreshment of the company".

Lady's Well

Today's visitor to Mulhuddart Church will but see the lower section of a squat tower and parts of the wall that once made up the nave. This is all that remains, yet even the casual observer cannot but notice that this was once an imposing edifice.

Little is know of the early history of the church. Then, in the 15th century 'the guild and fraternity of Our Lady of St Mary of the church of Mulhuddart' was formed. This was a religious guild, and was open to both women and men. It was also very prosperous, and this no doubt explains why the original church was a substantial building. The church was in good repair when the Royal Visitation took place in 1615, but a mere 15 years later Archbishop Bulkeley reported that both the chancel and nave were in ruins. He does not tell us what happened in the intervening years.

It is thought, however, that the church remained partially roofed for some considerable time. This is bourne out by the many reports of soldiers finding shelter there. During the Civil War of 1641-49 the contending armies marched through the area and laid much of it to waste. In 1643 the Royalist Earl of Cavan found shelter in the church for several days with a large troop of soldiers. Then, in 1648 Sir Francis Willoughby garrisoned the church with 77 men.

Isaac Butler refers to a massacre which occurred at the church in 1690 in the 'Journey to Lough Derg':

"In it was committed a most barbarous and infamous action by some of the neighbouring inhabitants in September, 1690. A company of Col. Foulke's men, in their march to Dublin, by stormy, rainy weather, retreated into the church for shelter, but all the them were murdered in cold blood before morning. Some of the wretches were afterwards executed in Thomas Street, Dublin."

Mulhuddart Churchyard

There has been a church on this site since early Christian times. It was rebuilt in 1605, and over the next 200 years was in various states of disrepair. By 1803 its condition was so bad that it had to be both rebuilt and enlarged.

Down through the years the church has had its share of characters. Dr Ralph Sadleir was one such. He served as vicar for over 50 years and, was described by his niece Winifred M Letts, as follows:

"What an imposing old man he was in his red robe, his white head shaking slightly, his manner that of one who commands his own church and congregation too".

More recently the Rev Paul Coulton, who was appointed Bishop of Cork, Cloyne and Ross in 1999, left a most valuable legacy for local historians. He drew up a list of the records of the parish from 1699-1984. Among the miscellaneous volumes is the Minute Book of the Farmers Society for the Union of Castleknock, '1797-1805'.

Stained Glass window (St Hubert) in St Brigid's Church

The minutes remind us of changes which have taken place in the area. The aims of the society were to improve agriculture in the area, and the *"encouraging and rewarding of faithful, industrious and sober servants and labourers"*. It encouraged the industrious poor *"during the summer months when they can earn most to pay up something against the time of need"*. This money would be collected on Sunday mornings *"because on that day the labourer can best spare time to look forward for the future comfort of his family"* and *"will feel less inclination to spend another sixpence idly at the alehouse"*.

The tomb of the Rev John Stone can be seen inside the Church's main entrance gate. Curate of St Michan's, Dublin, came to Castleknock to minister to victims of Typhus during the famine. He himself contracted the disease and died.

Within the church is a magnificent window by the Irish stained-glass artist Harry Clarke. It illustrates St Hubert, the patron saint of hunters, with St George to his right and St Luke to his left.

St Brigid's Church, Castleknock

The site of Castleknock Castle was well chosen by the Norman, Hugh Tyrrell. It was built on two mounds near the end of the esker which stretches from Galway to Dublin. The esker, known as the *Eiscair Riada*, is the highest point between the rivers Liffey and Tolka. As such it commanded the route into Dublin from the west.

Tyrrell was descended from a long line of nobles, and this is said to be the reason he was granted Castleknock, rather than any act of valour. One of his forefathers fought with distinction at Hastings in 1066. Another, Walter Tyrrell, was the archer who accidentally killed the hated William Rufus, successor to William the Conqueror, while hunting.

The polygonal keep was the notable feature of the castle. Attached to it was a large squat building. A curtain wall, interspersed with towers, surrounded the castle.

Castleknock Castle was the scene of many bloody encounters. One of these is recorded in a letter from an Irish officer to a friend in France, and refers to the year 1642:

"The Earl of Ormond, a Protestant, went forth from the City of Dublin .... At the head of 4000 foot and 500 horse towards the County Meath. The next day he besieged with his army Castleknock, belonging to the Lady de Lacy, aunt of the Earl of Fingal. The husband of this lady was engaged in the army of the Catholics of Ireland. He left his wife in the Castle to keep it with 50 men only, being well assured that her courage was well above her sex, in which he was not deceived, for this lady, by the orders she gave, caused 400 soldiers of the besiegers to be slain during the four days the siege lasted, and the number of dead would have been greater still, had not the ammunition failed ..."

The soldiers of the garrison set fire to the castle, and,

"all went down, sword in hand .... with the exception of the lady, who was made prisoner by the Earl of Ormond".

Castleknock Castle

In 1834 the Vincentian Fathers bought about 40 acres of land in Castleknock for their new school. The fields enclosed in this land were named Castle Field, Windmill Field, Limekiln Field and Hop Field. The land included two mounds or hills which were part of the esker known as the *Eiscair Riada*. On one of these mounds stood the remains of Castleknock Castle. The other had a tower.

The tower is built on Windmill Hill, so people assumed it had been a Windmill in days of old. However there is no record to suggest such a use. Some say it was used as a lime kiln, and that is a possibility, although why it would be built upon a hill, thereby creating a lot more work, has not been explained.

The Dublin Penny Journal, 1834, informs us that:

"Outside the town of Castleknock, and situated in the Demesne of Mr Guinn, are two steep hills, one a plain circular knoll, formally called Windmill Hill, crowned by a circular building, which was erected by Mr Guinn for an observatory, but afterwards let go to ruin"

Today the tower contains a water tank.

The Journal reports that the owner of the castle prior to Mr Guinn attempted to open a chamber under the entrenchments of the castle,

"and actually found a flight of steps leading to the vaults, when panic struck his labourers that the sleeping King (Morrishtac, the Dane – see page 68) might come upon them, and they instantly fled in the utmost confusion. The excavation was soon closed up. Money to an incredible amount is said to be buried in the Windmill Hill".

Windmill Hill

Travelling along the tree-lined Knocknamaroon Hill Road, high above the River Liffey, one suddenly comes to the entrance of an Anglo-Irish estate. The entrance is not spectacular, but the enormous clock tower, superseded by the even more enormous Lobb's Cypresses alert one to even greater grandeur behind the estate walls. One is not disappointed, for this is Farmleigh, the former home of the Guinness family. Farmleigh was not accessible to the public until recent times, and although this access is limited, this wonderful house and estate is now the property of the Irish people.

Farmleigh was bought in 1873 by Edward Cecil Guinness, who later became the 1st Earl of Iveagh. He employed the Irish Architect James F Fuller to remodel and alter the existing 18th century house, and this was completed by 1881. More additions were later made. The clock tower, familiar to generations of residents of the area, is in fact a pump house. Water is pumped up from the Liffey to the tank in

The Pump House at Farmleigh

the tower for use in Farmleigh. It was built in 1880.

Fuller also worked on the Guinness town house, at 80 St Stephen's Green (now Iveagh House and the Department of Foreign Affairs).

In 2000 the Guinness family decided it no longer required Farmleigh, and offered to sell it to the state for £23 million. The Government seized this opportunity, and Farmleigh is now to be used as a guesthouse for visiting Heads of State and foreign dignitaries. The Estate will be managed by the Office of Public Works, and they plan to open it to the public every summer. People can then enjoy its 78 acres of gardens, farmland, the ornamental lake, the majestic trees and sunken lawn, as well as the special events which will be organised.

Farmleigh House

In 1846 the Irish Ordnance Survey mapped *"every road and track every stone wall .... river .... house and barn"* in Ireland. This was the first time a whole country had been mapped, and it was done for the most odious of reasons - taxation. The county cess, or tax, was based on the value of each townland, so land boundaries had to be accurate. Hence map-making, which was completed at the Ordnance Survey office in the Phoenix Park.

Mapping in the 19th Century was not for the faint-hearted. Theodolites weighing 200lbs, measuring chains, water levels and limelights had to be hauled over the countryside. Field maps (plots) were drawn and later became *"printed maps by the careful eye and delicate touch of draughtsmen, engravers and printers, using quill pens and Chinese inks and copper plates"*.

One hundred and seventy five years on, mapping is totally unrecognisable. Techniques now include aerial surveying, global positioning, digitation and computerisation. And map makers have an eye for commercial opportunity. Today map making starts in the air. Two specially equipped aircraft, flying at a constant 5,000ft in a tight grid pattern, photograph the landscape with their 500lb specialist cameras. Parallel strips of photographs are taken with a 60 per cent overlap to ensure completeness. The roles of film are then scanned to the OSI Headquarters at very high resolution. Measurements from the photographs and the data from the field surveyors combine in a process known as photo-geometry to build up all the elements of geographical information.

So, who wants these high tech maps, and where is their commercial application? Banks and supermarkets use digital data showing every house in every area. This enables them to target their marketing campaigns. An Post uses its Geo directory, providing the national address file. In turn, this file will be used by the emergency services – ambulance, fire and Garda. And medical researchers are using geo-coding to identify clusters of illnesses. This is only the beginning of application, and it is all made happen in Luke Gardiner's old house (built in the 1730's) in Phoenix Park.

The Ordnance Survey of Ireland (OSI)

In 1989 an irate man wrote a letter to the Irish Times deploring the proposed demolition of the Papal Nunciature, one of the well known buildings in the Phoenix Park. The house was in fact riddled with dry rot, and there was no option but to demolish it. What happened next could not have happened in a more appropriate place than the Phoenix Park. As the house was being demolished the form of a castle appeared – out of the rubble, one might say, came Ashtown Castle.

The castle itself probably dates from the 1430s. At that time the government wanted the people of the Pale to take responsibility for their own protection and to this end awarded £10 to anybody who built a castle to specified dimensions. Ashtown Castle fits these dimensions.

In the late 1700s the castle was modernised and incorporated into a new building called Ashtown Lodge. In 1782 it became the official residence of the Under Secretary. One hundred years later the inhabitant of the Lodge, Thomas H Burke, was to meet a most brutal death. On the evening of the 6th May, Burke was on his way to the Viceregal Lodge (now Áras an Uachtaráin) to dine with the Viceroy, Lord Spencer. The other guest was Lord Frederick Cavendish, the newly appointed Chief Secretary of Ireland. Cavendish had decided to walk to the Viceregal Lodge and was almost there when Burke's cab drew up beside him. The two men decided to walk the remainder of the journey.

Lord Spencer, meantime, was reading some papers at a window overlooking the front of the Viceregal Lodge. He was suddenly startled by shrieks. The shrieks haunted him ever afterwards. They were the shrieks of Cavendish and Burke being hacked to death by the 'Invincibles', an extreme wing of the Fenians. The murderers were all later caught and hanged.

Ashtown Castle

The flat land to the west of the Magazine Fort is known to Dubliners as the Fifteen Acres. Well, so what if there is over 100 acres there – what would Dubliners know about land measurement? This ground has had many uses in its time – football and soccer pitches abound, and was not the first inter-county hurling match between South Galway and North Tipperary played here on February 12, 1886, refereed by Michael Cusack. The military used the Fifteen Acres for martial purposes, and so too did 18th century gentlemen to redeem their honour by duelling. The most noted duel fought here was that between the notorious Leonard McNally, the betrayer of Lord Edward Fitzgerald, and Sir Jonah Barrington.

"I was well aware of his object, and not feeling very uncomfortable under the insult, told him 'McNally, you shall meet me in the Park in an hour'".

Barrington continued,

"My second having stepped 9 paces then stood on the other side, handed me a pair of pistols, and desired me to work away. McNally stood before me, very like a beer-barrel on its stilling".

"McNally presented so cooly that I could see plainly that I had but little chance of being missed, so I thought it best to lose no time on my part. The poor fellow staggered and cried out ' I am hit'. Never did I experience so miserable a feeling."

He had been hit in the side, but the ball hit the buckle of his gallows (suspenders), and turned round instead of entering the body.

"As I was still in dread as to the result, my second, after seeing that he had been so far protected by his suspenders, inhumanly exclaimed, 'God, Mac! You are the only rogue I every knew that was saved by the gallows'".

Today duels are still fought on the Fifteen Acres but only by the park's stags each November!

The Fifteen Acres

"Behold a proof of Irish sense;
Here Irish wit is seen;
When nothing's left that's worth defence
We build a magazine".

So wrote Dean Swift of the Magazine Fort in the Phoenix Park. The Fort, perched high up on St Thomas's Hill, still gives one the sense of being watched by 'Big Brother'. Its solid granite walls protected by gun-turrets and an erstwhile moat and drawbridge, conveys an uneasy feeling to the modern passer-by. This grim-looking fort was built by Viceroy Wharton in 1734 as a storehouse for military ammunition. Because of this it was to be raided twice in the early 1900s.

About noon on Easter Monday 1916, seven volunteers arrived at the Fort by motor vehicle. Just a few soldiers were garrisoned the Fort, and when the sentry was disposed of, those in the guard house were quickly subdued. The Fort's other occupants were Mrs Playfair, the wife of the commandant who was at the front in France, and her two sons and daughter. She was seized by a volunteer who forced her to show him the telephone line, which he cut. She was then given six minutes to leave the Fort before it was blown up. The volunteers took whatever guns and ammunition they could carry and then set fire to the outer portion of the Fort. This contained small arms, *"and evidently being in a great hurry to get away, and unaware that the high explosives were stored in a different compartment, they fled the scene"* (1916 Rebellion Handbook). The fire was extinguished.

The second raid took place on December 23, 1939. It seems there was a festive atmosphere in the Fort, so when the IRA raiding party struck they encountered little resistance. The raiding party was well armed and organised, and was accompanied by 40 lorries. They took rifles, grenades and a million rounds of ammunition. However, the movement of such a convoy did not go unnoticed, and everything was recovered by the New Year.

The Magazine Fort

People love a hero so when Arthur Wellesley, Duke of Wellington reached that exalted height by his defeat of Napoleon in 1815, people in many places claimed association with him. In Ireland claimants argued for his place of birth as Dangan, Trim, Mornington, Athboy, Athy and Merrion Street, Dublin. A monument was built in his honour in the Phoenix Park. This monument is 205ft high. The pedestal is made up of panels showing battle scenes from his campaigns – Cuidad Rodrigo, Badajoz, Salamanca – cast in metal from canons captured from the French. Monuments such as this seem out of place today, but then it was erected at a time when power was in different hands.

The Wellesleys originally came from Somerset, arriving in Ireland in the 13th century. During the next 600 years their world in Ireland was the world of the coloniser.

One of the bronze sculptures on the testimonial. Wellington with Brittania to his right, Hibernia to his left.

"Behind him (ie Wellesley) *stretched an embattled English race who had occupied an alien land, marrying strictly with their own kind and becoming not only a ruling castle but a ruling garrison"* (Elizabeth Longford)

Wellesley was well acquainted with the condition of Ireland – at first that of the ascendancy, and in time the peasants. He was A.D.C. to the Lord Lieutenant, the Duke of Richmond, and there saw the 'rotten' state of the administration.

"He did little more than carry out the business placed in his hands, that is the management of elections, the dealing with patronage and the preparation of coercive measures" (O'Connor Morris).

Wellington was hostile to Catholic Emancipation but Daniel O'Connell's success in the Clare election, 1828, indicated to him that change was inevitable. Forty-shilling peasant freeholders had flexed the muscles of their Ireland, initiating the first step in a social revolution which would end the power of the landlords in 1881. Wellington died in 1852 and is buried in St Paul's, London.

The Wellington Testimonial

Owners of pets need little persuasion to convince them that animals have personalities of their own. Stories of eccentric dogs and cats, and indeed goats and pigs and others, abound. So the visitor to the zoo hopes, well really expects, to be entertained by unexpected displays of eccentric behaviour by the inhabitants of that institution.

On September 28, 1943 an editorial in the Irish Times was devoted to the antics of such a character in Dublin Zoo. Amid the chaos and carnage for control of Italy and the Russian advance to the Dnieper on the Eastern Front the paper announced to its readers that a pelican was missing from the zoo.

"Nobody would have suspected that beneath that staid and respectable exterior there beat a roamer's heart, his suave demeanour, his condensation to those visitors who paused to pass the time of day with him appeared to mark him out as the most sophisticated of birds-about-town. He was no common fowl requiring to be caged ... the gardens were free to him. He would stroll from the bear pit to the monkey house, or poke an affable bill into the warmth of the reptile house, with the contented look of a retired banker inspecting his dahlias. Occasionally he would permit himself the mild dissipation of a visit to Áras an Uachtaráin and frolic in the lake with the air of a privileged guest, but always he returned .... to the comfort and security of the zoo. Then, without any warning, the wanderlust came upon him and he was gone..... Romance had seized the feathered beast ..... his head full, no doubt, of romantic nonsense about warm springs and sunshine and fair, fascinating lady pelicans".

The Zoo was built in 1831 - when its sole inhabitant was a wild boar! The old entrance, a charming mock-Tudor cottage *orné* was designed by Decimus Burton, an English architect who worked on the Park from 1834 to 1849. He also designed the park gates.

The Zoo

Áras an Uachtaráin, the official residence of the President of Ireland, was originally built in 1751 as the lodge for the Park Ranger. Some years later a suitable residence was being sought for the Viceroy, and the lodge was purchased in 1782 for the sum of £10,000.

Initially rather small, three additions were considered necessary. The first of these was made by Robert Woodgate and later by Francis Johnston. They added the ballroom/state reception room and the wonderful south portico, giving the Áras the impression of an American 18th century colonial mansion. In 1849 Jacob Owen designed the dining room and the matching drawing room. Finally, between 1945-59 the East and West wings were reconstructed under OPW architect Raymond McGrath.

Strangely, had the Duke of Portland, the new Viceroy, had his way, this wonderful house would never have been built. Shortly after it was purchased Portland indicated that it was a 'white elephant', and he wanted to be rid of it.

"It was proposed to present the lodge and grounds to Henry Grattan, and thus associate the Crown with the people in doing honour to the illustrious author of the legislative liberties which has just been conceded to Ireland. So flattering an offer, conveyed in a manner so gracious, as the gift of the King's only palace in Ireland seemed likely for the moment to achieve the impossible,

and to unite the government and the people of Ireland in the person of Grattan".

But it was only for a moment. Sir Jonah Barrington analysed it thus:

"This magnificant and unexampled offer at first veiw, appeared flattering and showy, at second it appeared deceptious, and at third inadmissable"
(Barrington: '*Personal Recollections*')

The offer was declined.

Today the single window light representing the welcome home for Ireland's scattered emigrants, first lit by President Robinson in 1991, can be seen each night.

Áras an Uachtaráin

Dublin's main public park, the Phoenix Park, is said to be named after a spa which was located near the zoo. The word 'Phoenix' is thought to be a corruption of the Irish *Fionn Uisce* meaning 'clear water' which came from the spa.

Lord Chesterfield, the Viceroy from 1744-47, is the man who actually gave the park its Phoenix. He was a man of vision, wit, charm and tolerance. He saw the potential of the park and *"planted neatly arranged patterns of trees on its broad expanses, built a new road through it, and had the Phoenix Column – or the 'Ould Eagle' – grandly erected".* It is easy to imagine how some bemused Dubliner came to call this unfamiliar bird an eagle. The Phoenix itself was a mythical female bird said to have lived in Arabia. It is supposed to have lived for hundreds of years, and after burning itself, rose again from the ashes with fresh vigour.

The story of the Phoenix was known by republicans who adopted this bird as a symbol of the resurrection of a free Ireland. The Fenian, O'Donovan Rossa, had founded the Phoenix Society to help bring this about, and at his funeral in 1915 Pearse alludes to it directly:

"I hold it a Christian thing, as O'Donovan Rossa held it, to hate evil, to hate untruth, to hate oppression, and by hating them, to strive to overthrow them. Our foes are strong and wise ...... but they cannot undo the miracles of God who ripens in the hearts of young men the seeds sown ..... by the young men of '65. Rulers and defenders of realms had need to be wary if they would guard against such processes. Life springs from death, and from the graves of patriotic men and women spring living nations".

On the Phoeenix Monument are carved these words in Latin:

"For the pleasure of the general citizenry, this hitherto rough and uncultivated area of general ground was enhanced by Philip Stanhope, Count of Chesterfield, and Viceroy"

The Phoenix Monument

On Saturday December 20, 1919, the headlines in the Irish Times read:

MURDEROUS ATTACK NEAR ASHTOWN STATION
Thrilling story of his Excellency's escape

The Halfway House in Ashtown is a well-known hostelry on the Navan Road. It was here, on December 19, 1919, that an assassination attempt took place, which could have caused acute embarrassment to the British Government. The intended victim was the King's representative in Ireland, Field-Marshall Sir John French.

In his book, 'My Fight for Irish Freedom', Dan Breen writes, *"The police and the military were but the tools of higher men. Their loss did not trouble Britain very much… Why, we asked ourselves, should we not strike at the very heads of the British Government in Ireland? Such action would arouse interest in Ireland's cause throughout the world".*

In all, twelve ambushes were planned to assassinate Lord French, none of which succeeded. Then, in mid-December information was received that Lord French would return to Dublin, on Friday, December 19, from his estate at French Park, Co Roscommon. He would alight at Ashtown Station. This was

Memorial to Martin Savage opposite the pub

the opportunity the volunteers wanted, and they quickly organised for it. Their plan was to attack the second car in the convoy taking Lord French from the station to the Viceregal lodge. It was Lord French's custom to travel in the second car.

A party of eleven volunteers took up their positions. The train arrived on time and the first car passed. Unknown to the volunteers it carried Lord French. Immediately a farm cart was pushed out onto the narrow road to block the second car. Just before it was in position the second car arrived, backed up by the military escort. A fierce gunfight followed leaving three volunteers, Keogh, Savage and Breen, isolated behind the cart. Unexpectedly, another car came rushing towards the station. At this point Breen had been shot in the leg and Martin Savage killed. Keogh and Breen knew they could be trapped, so they dashed to the corner of Kelly's 'Halfway House' for shelter amidst a hail of bullets. When all seemed lost the shooting stopped and the troops withdrew. Breen concluded, *"with a prayer for the soul of our departed comrade, we mounted our bicycles and faced for the city".*

The Halfway House

The Dublin Institute for Advanced Studies houses its Astronomy Section of the School of Cosmic Physics at Dunsink Observatory. The Observatory can be seen as one travels towards Dublin to the north of the Navan Road.

The Observatory, founded in 1785, was the brainchild of two Trinity College men, the Provost Dr Francis Andrews and the Rev Dr Henry Ussher. Dr Andrews was so enthusiastic that he left £2,000 in his will for the project as well as £250 per annum for the salaries of the astronomer and his assistants. Although this was a large sum it was not sufficient and the Board of Trinity College provided the additional £5,500 needed.

The plans for the Observatory were drawn up by Dr Ussher, a recognised authority on astronomical matters and a noted scientist. He chose Dunsink as the site for the Observatory as it had the necessary advantages – it is built on the top of a hill giving it an uninterrupted view of the horizons in all directions. Cloudy weather, of course, would cause a problem, but the Dublin-Wicklow mountains to the south could help minimise that by acting as a barrier to the south-westerly rain-bearing winds.

The Observatory itself was a two-storey building with a dome. The main telescope was mounted in the dome, fixed on a block of masonry which rested on the solid rock beneath the building. All the Observatory's telescopes were made by the renowned instrument maker Jesse Ramsden.

Sadly, Dr Ussher's tenure at Dunsink ended abruptly in 1790. It is said he caught a chill while working at night in the unheated dome.

Down through the years outstanding people worked at Dunsink, but pride of place must surely go to William Rowan Hamilton. A child prodigy, he had a brilliant career in science, poetry and the classics. At the age of 21 he was appointed Professor of Astronomy and Astronomer Royal of Ireland. Hamilton loved walking in the countryside around Dunsink, and entertained his friend William Wordsworth, the poet there. He regularly walked from Dunsink into the city. In October 1843 as he walked along the Royal Canal he stopped at Broome Bridge and worked out his mathematical theory of Quaternions. A plaque on the bridge commemorates the event.

Dunsink Observatory

The People

In 1983 a man was digging his garden in Clonsilla when he noticed a stone that looked out of place. The man, Miley Caldwell, sent it to the National Museum where it was found to be a finely polished stone axe-head dating from the New Stone Age. The Museum made a replica of the axe-head and gave it to Miley, who in turn gave it to Coolmine Community School. This find suggests that people lived in the area during Neolithic times, although no further evidence has emerged of these settlers.

The Celts were the first to leave their imprint on the landscape between the Liffey and the Tolka in West Dublin. The remains of nine raths, or ringforts, are still evident. These raths were farmsteads, housing on average seven people. The rath itself was a level area enclosed by a circular earthen bank and fosse (ditch), with a diameter varying from 50ft to 100ft. A stockade or wooden fence was built on top of the earthen bank to give extra protection. The Celts who inhabited these raths were primarily pastoral farmers, but did practice tillage farming too. Possibly the best example of these raths is the one found in Corduff

Park. Good examples are also found at Dunsink, Buzzardstown, Cappoge and Castleknock, while those at Dainstown and Astagob have disappeared. The 'rath' at Coolmine has a different origin. It was, in fact, the site of St Mochta's Church.

During the Celtic period two battles were fought at Castleknock. The second of these is mentioned in the Book of Ballymote. It seems that Cumhal, father of the famed Fionn Mac Cumhail, abducted Muireann Munchaomh 'The fairest woman in Eirinn', and daughter of the druid of Allen. He asked the High King of Ireland, Conn of the Hundred Battles, for help to recover his daughter. The High King asked Cumhal to release Muireann, but was ignored. This insult obliged Conn to take military action, and with the aid of Goll Mac Morna of Connaught he defeated and killed Camhal at Castleknock.

St Patrick is said to have visited the area circa 450AD and made many converts. The following account of his visit was given in The Dublin Penny Journal, 1834:

"Patrick… came to Castlenoc, then in the possession of a Danish King, called Morrishtac, whom he endeavoured to convert, but the Dane, not wishing to be bothered by the pious saint, and unwilling to be inhospitable, after listening for some time, and giving sundry nods of approval… at length fell asleep in his great armchair. St Patrick preached on for some time, until he was astounded by a most unchristian snore from the poor Dane, and then his rage knew no bounds. He tore his beard and acted several ramashes, and in the height of his passion, prayed that the uncircumcised King should sleep in the same place and posture till the day of judgement".

The first Christian Church in the area was founded by St Mochta at Coolmine. This gave Coolmine a certain prestige as Mochta was the last of St Patrick's disciples and also the Abbot of Louth. And of course many miracles were performed by him. One recalls the robber who was condemned to death by King Ailill. The robber's parents begged Mochta to ask the King for leniency, but Ailill refused to change his mind. The robber had a large stone suspended from his neck and was then thrown into the sea. When his body was recovered Mochta raised him to life. Later, the robber converted and became a monk. According to the Annals of the Four Masters Mochta died on August 19, 534 AD. His Church at Coolmine served as the Parish Church until the late 1400s, but by 1490 it had completely disappeared.

There is no record of a Church in Castleknock at this time, but it does seem likely that there was one. In 1185 Richard Tyrrell, son of Castleknock's first Baron, Hugh Tyrell, gave a grant of land to Benedictine monks at Castleknock to re-edify the Church of St Brigid's, Castleknock.

In 1938 a graveyard, dating from the 10th century, was discovered in a field north of Castleknock and close to the Tolka. Objects found in the cemetery were characteristic of the culture of the early Christian period in Ireland, a few bronze pins, amber beads and a bronze shoe buckle. We even know a little as to how these people looked from their skeletal remains; these remains also give some indication of their lifestyle. They were of moderate stature with well-built frames in comparison with the rest of the population. The skulls of these skeletons revealed considerable wear from the crushing of their teeth. This indicated the gritty nature of the food eaten, probably corn ground in a quern. The deltoid muscle in many of the humeri, of the skeletons showed exceptional development. This is best seen in the arm bones of those who use slings, most likely in hunting. The stout short feet of the skeletons indicated adaptations to heavy work associated with tillage and hunting. Bearing all of this in mind we do know that the rath dwellers of Celtic and Christian Ireland were primarily pastoral farmers and hunters.

The arrival of the Normans in 1169 was to change the political face of West Dublin for most of the next 800 years. The Norman leader, Strongbow, had taken Dublin and assumed the title 'King of Leinster'. Archbishop O'Toole was so shocked at this development that he travelled all over Ireland in an attempt to rouse the Irish chieftains into action. He was successful and the country rose in support. Under the leadership of the High King, Rory O'Connor, 30,000 men, mainly from Connaught, laid siege to Dublin. At the same time a fleet under Gottred, King of Man, blocked the port. O'Connor set up his headquarters at Castleknock. His aim was to starve the Normans into submission. After two months the Norman's supplies began to run out. Becoming desperate, Strongbow sent Maurice de

Prendergast to seek terms from O'Connor. He offered to become the High King's subject and hold Leinster for him. O'Connor saw this as weakness and would only offer the towns of Dublin, Waterford and Wexford. When de Prendergast returned he was able to report on the state of O'Connor's military preparedness – things were very lax. In fact some of the Irish forces were raiding in South Leinster while others were off destroying crops to prevent supplies reaching Dublin.

The Normans saw this as their opportunity. Under the cover of darkness three companies, led by Strongbow, Miles de Cogan and Raymond Le Gros, slipped out of Dublin. Each company had about 200 men made up of knights, archers and foot soldiers.

De Cogan's company headed for Finglas and then turned south-west for Castleknock. At the same time the other two companies approached Castleknock directly, using the Stoneybatter Road. At daybreak the Normans attacked. They caught the Irish completely off guard and soon routed them. The pursuit lasted until evening when the victorious Normans returned to Dublin laden with supplies.

The Normans now controlled Dublin and its

hinterland, causing alarm to King Henry II. He was afraid that Strongbow might try to set up a rival Norman Kingdom in Ireland, so to prevent this happening he granted the land from Dublin to the Shannon to Hugh de Lacy, one of his own followers. De Lacy in turn granted the fort and lands at Castleknock to his friend Hugh Tyrrell, as well as Clonsilla, Mulhuddart, Ward, Cloghran and much of the Phoenix Park. Thus the Barony of Castleknock came into being.

Hugh Tyrrell, the 1st Baron of Castleknock, was descended from a long line of nobles. He himself had done nothing spectacular, but one of his forefathers had fought with great distinction at Hastings in 1066. Another, Walter Tyrrell, was the archer who killed the hated William Rufus, successor of William the Conqueror. William was killed while hunting and while there was a debate whether his death was accidental or otherwise, few tears were shed at his demise.

Tyrrell chose the most strategic site in the Barony for his castle. The site has two mounds, which are part of the *Eiscair Riada*, which stretches from Galway to Dublin. The most striking feature of the castle was its polygonal keep on one of these

mounds. The keep also formed part of the outer defence. Such keeps were not common in Ireland, but equally so were not unknown. The castles at Dungargan, Co Waterford and Shanid, Co Limerick possess similar keeps.

By the end of the 13th century the area was heavily anglicisied. One has merely to look at the number of townlands, which had added the suffix 'town' to local Anglo-Norman patronymics to get a sense of conquest. Examples are Porterstown, Huntstown, Tyrrellstown, Buzzardstown and of course, Blanchardstown. Even the townlands which retained Irish names were in the possession of Anglo-Normans; the De La Felde family, for example, possessed Corduff while the Sheriff of Dublin, John Woodlock, owned Cappoge.

The change in the political system was soon reflected in the agricultural system introduced by the Anglo-Normans. Their open field system of farming emphasised the production of grain, and before long 81% of the land was given over to tillage. Mills appeared at Castleknock, Corduff and Luttrellstown.

Rural village life in the barony had its moments of excitement. A forger from Blanchardstown, Philip

Cowherd, claimed he had deeds to various estates near Castleknock. He sold these to, *"People who knew not the law, and who from one day to another menaced the tenants and freeholders"*. Parliament had to be invoked to cancel the deeds.

Even the aristocracy caused headlines. John Tyrrell, brother of Richard, the 6th Baron, was gaoled for causing a disturbance. He disliked the Deuswells so much that he attacked John Deuswell as he and his brother Hugh sat in the garden. Hugh drew his dagger and drove Tyrrell off. Tyrrell returned to the castle where he armed himself, mounted a war-horse and sought out the Deuswells. When he found them at their mother's home he unsuccessfully tried to force his way in. So he dismounted and began to throw stones at the house. *"Unless Tyrrell was prevented by the hue and cry raised by which the neighbours of those parts came, there he would have done much evil"*. (O'Discoll, J. 'Cnucha')

February 1317 was an eventful date in the annals of West Dublin. Edward Bruce, brother of Robert, King of Scotland, stopped at Castleknock with an army of 20,000 soldiers. He had been crowned King of Ireland in May 1316, and now his aim was to take Dublin. His army had to be fed off the country, so one assumes that the people of the area had their goods plundered. Bruce succeeded in capturing the Baron, Hugh Tyrrell, and his wife and only released them when a ransom was paid. The same night Dubliners set fire to the houses around Thomas Street to prevent the Scots availing of cover when they commenced their attack on the city. This determination from the citizens impressed Bruce, and when he observed the city's solid fortications he needed little convincing to move on. He marched towards Naas and then Limerick, but first turned aside to Leixlip *"where he remained four days, burning and plundering"*.

When the Reformation parliament met in 1536-7 to approve King Henry VIII's policies for Ireland, all the members were Old English from the Pale. Their task caused them anxiety as it placed them in an unwanted dilemma. As a class they were loyal to the Crown and could be depended on in political matters. But in religious matters they were loyal to the Church of Rome. The new legislation, which Henry wished to introduce, exacerbated this dilemma. They were slow to oppose his wishes, and needed no reminder of the consequences should they fail to please the King. They were still shocked by the treatment meted out to the Fitzgeralds of Kildare. Yet their consciences made them reluctant to recognise Henry as Head of the Church of Ireland.

Browne, the new Archbishop of Dublin, knew how to deal with these qualms – intimidation - *"He who will not pass this act as I do is no true subject of his Majesty"*. The threat worked and the Act of Supremacy was passed. An Act against the authority of the Bishop of Rome, also passed, reinforced them in their view of Tudor determination. This act declared that anybody who supported the Pope's claim to be head of the Church would be outlawed and have all their property confiscated. This had the desired effect – land and property are deeply engrained in the Irish psyche. Parliament also ordered the closure of the monasteries, and within five years all monasteries in the Pale had ceased to exist. True to character the lords who were reluctant to accept royal supremacy showed no such hesitancy in accepting monastic lands. These included Sir Thomas Luttrell, the Chief Justice, who received Church lands in Clonsilla and Coolmine, John Alen in Tipperstown, and Murrogh, Earl of Thomand, at Coolmine and Ravelston. The Chapel at Coolmine was stripped of its gold, silver and plate to the value of £9, while the Parish Church of Castleknock lost £18.

The mid 17th century was a bloody period in Irish history involving Gaelic Irish, Old English, Royalists and Cromwell's Parliamentarians.

"The scenario is one of endless on-off war with shifting lines, wandering detachment, often at cross-purpose with each other, bewildering kaleidoscopes of alliances ….. and sudden changes of side, and a blood letting that both invoked and reinforced the bitterest religious dissensions." (Roy Foster).

In 1641 England was on the verge of civil war. The King, Charles I, and parliament were heading towards war, allowing Sir Phelim O'Neill to see this as an opportunity to rebel against English rule. The Old English were faced with a difficult choice. Should they side with the English Government which distrusted them as they were Catholics, and could not be depended on to defend their property, or should they join forces with the Gaelic Irish, their fellow Catholics? Both groups declared their loyalty to Charles, but in order to defend their lands and religion they united in a common cause. Known as the "Confederate Catholics of Ireland" they had their headquarters at Kilkenny. By so organising they committed high treason and quite a number of men from this area were declared outlaws by the King's bench. Included were Edward Beringham and Richard Engle, Coolmine; George Fleming, Blakestowne; James, John and Richard Long, Abbotstowne; Thomas and William Casie, John Ratty and Thomas Wade, Courtduffe (Corduff); and John Warren and Christopher Burnell, Castleknock. Burnell owned Castleknock Castle, and because of its strategic position in relation to Dublin, which was controlled by the Royalists, it was a threat to the safety of the city. In May 1642, the Royalists, under the command of Lt Thomas Bringhurst, attacked it, but made no headway. A month later General Monck captured it. The castle was defended by Lady Lacy whose rousing speech harangued her soldiers thus:

"My faithful servants, you can well judge by the action I am after performing, what hope there is of favour from our enemies, and how little clemency I expect at their hands…. You should not expect quarter from them, but remember the sentence which says 'let the vanquished hope for nothing from their enemies'. Take courage then, and combat to death for the faith of your Redeemer; you can never find a more glorious end, and the sooner to find it, go valiantly to attack the enemy of the cross, lest, being made prisoners, any of you should, by

bad treatment or the violence of torments, fail in the good resolution you have taken of dying today for the Catholic faith". (Ms. 11657, N.L.I.)

She then set fire to the castle. The defenders killed 400 of the attackers and would have killed more had the ammunition not failed. They then *"went down sword in hand".* The castle took a terrible pounding from cannon and its structure was badly damaged.

In October 1646 the Confederate Generals, Preston and O'Neill planned an attack on Dublin, *"the Metropolis of the Kingdom, the enemies great magazine of all provisions for the war".* By November they had their headquarters at Lucan, 6 miles from Dublin, where *"the soldiers ….. made booty of all that happened in their way".* These words were written by Sir Richard Belling of Mulhuddart, an historian and officer in the war in his great work 'The History of the Irish Government and the War in Ireland 1641-1649'. He does not mention how this area was affected. Folklore relates that O'Neill took possession of the area before deciding not to proceed towards Dublin. In the process he destroyed *"the goodliest haggards of corn that ever were seen in those parts".*

One of the consequences of the war was the growth

of the wolf population. In times of peace the nobility controlled these creatures during hunts. There were no hunters now and the Scaldwood, the great wood of Blanchardstown, was the breeding ground for an increasing wolf population. Things were so serious that the Government, in 1652, ordered a public hunt in which people from the Barony were ordered to participate.

Following the surrender of Dublin to the parliamentary army in 1647 the Luttrells were forced to leave their estate and live in their Dublin townhouse. They were royalists and it was known that Simon Luttrell had waited on King Charles at Oxford. *"Luttrellstown was too attractive a possession to escape the eyes of the new rulers of Ireland, and was quickly seized upon…. By Colonel John Hewson, who had been appointed Governor of Dublin"*. Described as *"one of the most unrelenting of the regicides"*, he was not around long enough to enjoy his spoils. He was forced to flee to the continent after the restoration. Fortunately for the Luttrells they were close friends of the Duke of Ormonde, and he was instrumental in helping them have their castle and estates returned in the Act of Settlement (1663). After an unsteady initial period the Luttrell star rose, and for the next

150 years they were to play a prominent role in Irish affairs.

In 1685 King Charles II died and was succeeded by his brother, James. James was a Catholic, and while English and Irish Protestants were alarmed, they were prepared to accept him, as his heir was his daughter Mary, a Protestant. Mary was married to William of Orange. In 1688 James aroused a furious outcry when he removed the Penal Laws against both Catholics and Dissenters. This was exacerbated when his son was born, thereby giving rise to a potential line of Catholic rulers. Powerful interests in England could not tolerate this, and invited William of Orange and his wife Mary to become rulers of England.

In the same year war broke out in Europe between King Louis XIV of France, and a league of European states led by William. These states aimed to curtail Louis's expansionist plans. Louis hoped to keep William busy in Ireland, and away from Europe, by supplying James with money, weapons and men.

The aristocratic families of the Pale gave immediate support to King James. These included the Luttrells. Colonel Simon Luttrell was appointed Governor of

Dublin, and he proceeded to prepare the city against attack by *"chaining up the streets and making breast-works in order to secure that naked place"*. He also raised a regiment of dragoons for the King and then appears to have gone to France, where he died in 1698. His brother, Colonel Henry Luttrell, succeeded him.

Henry Luttrell was a notorious character who brought much dishonour to his family name. He spent his early life in France, and in the year 1684 alone he fought three duels, in which he was wounded and one of the combatants killed. He returned to Ireland to serve King James, and *"brought back… a sharpened intellect and polished manners, a flattering tongue, some skills in war, and much more skills in intrigue"* (Macaulay). Luttrell fought bravely on the side of King James and his success over the enemy cavalry at Enniskillen was of significance. At Aughrim (1691) he commanded four regiments of dragoons which were forced to retreat – this was wrongly interpreted later as an act of treachery.

The Jacobite commander Saint-Ruth chose Aughrim as his site for engaging the Williamites because of its hill and bogs. He arranged his army so that the Williamites could only attack across the causeway through the village of Aughrim, or across the ford on the other side of the hill of Kilcommodon. To prevent these attacks he placed a division of cavalry and dragoons opposite each of these approaches, thereby forcing them to attack across the bog. A small ruined, but sturdy, castle controlled the causeway. Here Colonel Walter Burke commanded 200 musketeers. Behind him two infantry regiments were positioned to prevent the English cavalry crossing, and behind them brigadier Henry Luttrell commanded his dragoons.

During the battle these infantry were moved to reinforce the centre. Ginkel, the Williamite commander, spotted the weakness created by this move and the English cavalry were ordered to attack through the causeway. Burke's men were defending magnificently – then disaster struck. He had been issued with the wrong size musket balls and there was nothing he could do to stop the cavalry riding past the castle. Luttrell was left without any support, but no reinforcements came. He pulled his men back, and when fresh squadrons of English cavalry arrived over the causeway he knew his men were about to be wiped out. He had only one option – retreat off the battlefield.

Luttrell now seems to have had doubts about his loyalty, especially as he considered where his own personal interests lay. At Limerick he was found to be corresponding with the enemy, *"having made some proposals for the surrender of the place"* (W.A.P. Wauchopes). He was court marshalled and condemned to death. The English responded to the news, warning *"that if they put anyone to death for having a mind to come over to us he will revenge it on the Irish"*. On the surrender of Limerick, Luttrell openly went over to the Williamites, and was awarded with the ancestral estates, a pension of £500 a year, and was appointed Major General to a Dutch regiment in 1702.

Luttrell was hated in Ireland, so when he was assassinated in November 1717 few tears were shed. He was returning to his town house in Stafford Street by sedan chair when he was shot. Despite a reward of £100 by the Irish House of Commons nobody was ever charged with his murder. Hardiman's epigram reflects the low esteem in which he was held.

"If heaven be pleased when mortals cease to sin,
And hell be pleased when villains enter in,
If each be pleased when it entombs a knave,
All must be pleased – now Luttrell is in the grave".

The Warren brothers from Corduff played an active role in the war between Britain and France (1740-48). Captains William and John Warren fought with the regiment of Lally in the French victory at Fontenoy in 1745. They also fought on the side of Bonnie Prince Charlie, son of James Stewart and pretender to the throne, at Culloden, 1746. Yet it was their brother, Colonel Richard Warren, who is best remembered. He was in France negotiating the assistance of 6,000 French troops and financial aid, when the news of the defeat at Culloden reached him. A task force was immediately organised to rescue the Prince and Warren was selected to lead it. He landed in Scotland, eventually rendezvoused with Charlie and, after many hair breadth escapes, led the Prince to Skye and from there to France.

The English agricultural writer, Arthur Young toured Ireland in the mid 1770s, and as part of this tour he visited Luttrellstown (June 1776). He wrote,

"On June 24th I passed through the Phoenix Park, a very pleasing ground, at the bottom of which, to the left, the Liffey forms a variety of landscapes, this is the most beautiful environ of Dublin. Take the road to Luttrell's town through a various scenery on the banks of the river, that domain is a considerable

one in extent, being above 400 acres… in front of the house is a fine lawn bounded by rich woods… Lord Irnham and Colonel Luttrell have brought in the assistance of agriculture to add to the beauties of the place".

He went on to praise the farming methods employed, especially the use of limestone and the type of drains. In particular he mentions the form of crop rotation practised in Co Dublin:

1. Fallow.
2. Wheat. Sow 1 barrel and get an average of 8 barrels.
3. Oats. Sow 2 barrels and get from 12-20.
4. Clover. Sometimes sown after oats.

And he makes some general comments on the social condition of the area:

"Most people drink tea, and consume plenty of whiskey and tobacco… rent of cottages 26s to 30s with a potato garden. No emigration. The religion in general Catholic. Labour through the year 10d a day, about Dublin 1s".

Some provision costs were: *"bread, 10lb in weight*

cost 12d, bacon 6d, new milk 2d a quart, potatoes 1s 6d per cwt, candles 5¹/₂d per lb, soap 6d, firing all stolen."*

In November 1797 a Farmers' Society for the Union of Castleknock was formed. It had two principle aims,

1. The improvement of agriculture in the area,
2. The encouraging and rewarding of faithful, industrious and sober servants and labourers.

Over the years reports were given on farm machinery, cattle breeding and fertilisers. In 1801 the society was informed that there was a threshing machine on Mr McFarland's farm. The same meeting also reported that:

"Mr Wynn had imported two fine cows of the Leicestershire breed. He has also hired at great price and brought over an English bull with some other gentlemen".

At its meeting in April 1803 the society saw the need:

"to encourage the industrious poor… during the

summer months when they can earn most to lay up something against the time of need".

To encourage savings the members agreed to add ¼ of any sum saved by the afore mentioned. Subscribers would be asked to make their contributions on a Sunday morning,

"because on that day the labourer can best spare time to look forward for the future comfort of his family, will feel the less inclination to spend another sixpence idly at the alehouse".

Henry Grattan wrote,

"From the close of 1795 the country was in a state of war, the people in rebellion against the King, the Minister against the Constitution".

Yet in 1792 citizens from Castleknock, Leixlip, Chapelizod and Dunboyne found it necessary to set up the Association for the Protection of Property. Frequent outrages and offences were the cause. Members complained of the *"barbarous practice of killing sheep for the purpose of stealing their fat only"**. A particularly vicious crime was carried out against the widow Tiernan. She was robbed and raped. The criminals were pursued by Major William Brady. The only suspect, a Patrick Daly, was acquitted, but later Daniel Leals, *"a most notorious offender"** was charged and lodged in Kilmainham Gaol. The Association gave the widow £20 compensation. Numerous robberies were carried out between 1798-1800 by armed bandits, and the situation was so bad by 1800 that calls were made for a constable to be appointed who could *"call upon members to give immediate assistance"**. In August 1800 one of Luttrell's lodges was attacked by armed men and Stewart Byrne was robbed of his gun. A reward of £50 was offered.

At a national level, a new Commander in Chief of His Majesty's forces was appointed for Ireland in 1795 - Henry Lawes Luttrell, the Earl of Carhampton. The Government faced both internal and external threats and responded by adopting a policy of repression. This was supported by the Insurrection Act, 1796. The country was deemed to be in a state of insurrection so a curfew was imposed. Carhampton enthusiastically undertook to suppress all opposition and seems to have chosen West Dublin/North Kildare as an example, inflicting acts of cruelty on its population. Two men from

* Quotes from the Association's minute book.

Clonsilla; James Dunn, a blacksmith, and Pat Casey, were so enraged with Carhampton's actions that they asked the Strand Street Committee of the United Irishmen for help to assassinate him. They planned to kill him the following Sunday, May 7, 1797, when he visited Luttrellstown after church at Kilmainham. Dunn told the committee that he could get a blunderbuss and pistols from a pawnbroker in Dorset Street, but that he and Carthy would need money from them to escape from Ireland. Later that evening the committee agreed to help, and had no sooner broken up than its chairman, James Ferris, sent a message to Carhampton at Kilmainham Hospital informing him of events.

By Tuesday, May 3rd, Duigenan, the Treasurer of the United Irishmen, had failed to produce the money so the plot was cancelled. On Sunday evening, the day when the assassination was to have taken place, Dunn and Carthy were arrested and imprisoned in Kilmainham Gaol. Although Dunn confessed they were both tortured. Carhampton actually came to Kilmainham to cross-examine them on three occasions, accompanied by Lord Enniskillen. They gouged out one of Dunn's eyes. The two men were tried and convicted of treason against the Commander of His Majesty's Forces.

They were hanged, drawn and quartered at the corner of Strand Street and Jervis Street, on November 11, 1797, watched by an immense crowd.

When the rebellion of 1798 failed, the grave of Lord Carhampton's Grandfather, Colonel Henry Luttrell, was burst open in Clonsilla Churchyard and his skull was smashed open with a pickaxe. Carhampton died in London in 1821 and neither he nor any other Luttrells were buried in Clonsilla. The name Luttrell was now so odious in West Dublin that the new owner of Luttrellstown, Luke White, changed its name to Woodlands.

In 1798 Parliament granted permission to construct the Royal Canal. The canal would run from Dublin to the Shannon, via Mullingar, a distance of 109 miles. The estimated cost was £197,098, and Parliament offered a grant of £66,000 towards the cost. The man behind the venture was a Mr Binns, and he had powerful backers in the Duke of Leinster, the Earl of Carhampton, Lord Longford and Alexander Kirkpatrick of Coolmine. The canal seemed to be an economically viable project on the surface, but one wonders if the shareholders knew that Binns' motives for building the canal were driven by revenge rather than financial gain. He had been a director of the Grand Canal Company and had invested a large sum of money in the company. He influenced company decisions, and it appears that on many occasions took decisions without consulting other board members. His actions were so unacceptable that the members banded together and out-voted him. After an acrimonious meeting Binns resigned, vowing revenge:

"You may think me a very insignificant person, but I will show you the contrary. I will sell out forthwith, start a rival canal, and carry all the traffic".

Within 50 years the Royal Canal was bought by the Midland and Great Western Railway who used its level banks to construct railway tracks.

On November 25, 1845, 17 people died in Ireland's worst canal disaster. The night boat to Longford left Dublin at 2.00pm with 47 passengers and 7 crew aboard. The evening was cold, dark and wet – not conducive to staying on the exposed deck. After the boat passed Porterstown Bridge the steersman, James Dunne, handed over the steering to a free traveller called Patrick Teeling. Teeling was under the influence of drink and steered the boat into the canal bank. The boat keeled over. The passengers rushed to the door in their panic to escape, but this action had the effect of further unbalancing the craft. Water poured in and quickly filled the boat. Passengers in the front cabin escaped, but those in the after cabin were not so fortunate. Local people gave whatever help they could, mainly sheltering those who were rescued. One person in particular was commended for his courage. A young soldier, Private Jessop of the 8th Hussars, was returning to his regiment in Longford. He is credited with saving a number of lives. The inquest into the disaster blamed three people. The Captain, (Christopher O'Connor), James Dunne and Patrick Teeling. The corner recommended that Teeling be committed for trial on a manslaughter charge.

The effects of the Great Famine (1845-49) seem to have been limited in this general area. People did die from hunger and hunger related illnesses, yet the evidence seems to suggest that many of those, although not all, would have died whether or not there was a famine. Fr Michael Dungan, Parish Priest of Blanchardstown, kept a diary of events in the parish and never once refers to the famine. An entry for January 19, 1846 simply records that the, *"Dairy broken into at night and meal, meat taken away"*.

There is no suggestion that the robbery was anything other than an attempt by a local person stealing in order to eat. Yet folk memory can be different. The Irish Folklore Commission has a child's account (written in the 1930s) of the famine in the Castleknock area. She writes:

"Any of the farmers that lived there had to sell their corn and cattle as payment for rent to the English landlords, so that when the famine did come the people were starved".

This sounds more like a political statement; the problem for these farmers was high rates, and not potato failure. The population given in the Census of 1841 for this area was 4,263 persons. There was obvious poverty here as 34.8% of the people lived in 4th class accommodation. This meant they lived in mud cabins with one single room. Relatively speaking this was a high percentage, yet the figures for destitute poor who went to the poorhouse in North Brunswick Street are low.

Year	1844	1845	1846	1847	1848	1849
Blanch'town	15	42	32	39	28	26
Castleknock	17	16	27	38	38	30

Some were old and ill, and of the total number 52 were children, including orphans.

An analysis shows that many people were admitted to the workhouse as they were unable to support themselves. Then, when the authorities considered they were well enough to face the world again they were discharged. Many returned at a later date.

The Earl family is an example. They arrived in the workhouse for the first time on May 20, 1844. The family consisted of Thomas (42), Cathern (41) and their 4 children, James (10), Alicia (7), Cathern (6) and Thomas (17 months). Thomas, a labourer, was suffering from *"disease of the knee"*, while the whole family were in a *"ragged"* condition. They were discharged on October 8th. It is interesting to note that they were admitted during the *"hungry months"*. They returned to the workhouse on March 23, 1845, but this time with only two children, Alicia and Cathern. The children had *"very delicate chests"* and Thomas was suffering from *"bad epestaxis"*. They left the workhouse on August 18th but returned a week later. This time Thomas senior and junior were not admitted, but there was a new arrival, seven month old Esther. On May 18, 1846, Thomas senior was readmitted, and two months later the whole family left.

The death rate rose during the Famine years as shown by the figures recorded by Fr Dungan.

Year	1846	1847	1848	1849	1850	1851	1852
No. of deaths	74	105	88	133	61	48	42

The figures do suggest that there was a rise in the death rate during the Famine years. Assuming that the annual death rate was about 50 then the increases are noticeable, especially in 1847 and 1849. The cause of death in the majority of cases in the east of Ireland was disease, *"brought by migrant workers of people planning to emigrate. This would account for the increase of deaths from 1846-48"* (John Gleeson). This, in turn, suggests that some of those who died might not be natives of the area. Then, in 1849, there was a cholera epidemic and this would explain the increased number of deaths in that year. These figures are disturbing, yet compared with the western seaboard of Ireland they are light. One must conclude, then, that the famine had limited effects in this locality.

Finally, the 1851 census does reflect Fr Dungan's figures, and shows a decrease in population of 308 persons, or 7%, yet not all of these would have died. Emigration would account for part of the decrease. The census also tells us where the decrease came. The group to suffer most was the poorest class, those who lived in 4th class accommodation. In 1851 only 8.2% of the houses in the area were in this category, compared with 34.8% in 1841 and, the number of houses in the 3rd class, 2nd class and 1st class accommodation increased. The unexpected conclusion one draws is that people, in general, experienced a rise in living standards, and at the same time it demonstrated the limited effect the famine had in the locality.

The royal visit by Queen Victoria in 1900 caused a certain amount of excitement in West Dublin. The Queen and her party resided at the Viceregal Lodge in the Phoenix Park, and from there made excursions into the countryside. One was to Lucan, and on the return journey to the Park the Royal party travelled via the Strawberry Beds. On Sunday, April 22nd the Queen visited Castleknock College.

"Three ringing cheers greeted the arrival of the royal carriage, and the aged Queen bowed her gracious acknowledgements", wrote the college chronicle of

June 1900.

Yet, the Royal visit was not without controversy. Ireland was undergoing a cultural and political revival, so reaction to the visit was vocal. One of the emotive outbursts concerned the organisation of a party for children. It was to be held in the Phoenix Park and attended by the Queen. Invitations were extended through city and county schools and institutions to the poor working class children, both Catholic and Protestant, to attend a charity picnic, which would be attended by the Queen. Some Catholic clergy saw this as a return to 'souperism' and reacted accordingly. On March 28th a letter was published in the Freeman's Journal in which the writer refers to one Dublin school where the children refused the invitation.

"Many of those children were barefooted and extremely poor, nevertheless, their parents had too much of the noble Irish pride to accept of a 'charity feast' for their little ones, and which they believed was only calculated to degrade them. Nor was this owing to any feeling of personal disrespect to Her Majesty, who, if she came over in the capacity of a private visitor, should not have awakened the disagreeable party feeling now prepared for her by the Jingoes".

The party went ahead and thousands of children attended. Various firms made donations towards the party; including Jacobs who contributed one ton of biscuits, William and Woods - one ton of jam and 10,000 bags of sweets, Downs - 1,800 buns, Hamilton Drummond - 2,500 oranges, Cleeve Brothers, Limerick, - 7cwt of butter, Shaw and Sons, Limerick, - 1,250lbs of ham, and Lucan Dairy - 300 gallons of milk.

On the artistic front, a co-operative stained-glass works was set up in Dundrum, Co Dublin in 1903. This was a response to the desire to get away from the mass-production techniques of the industrial revolution and re-establish hand craftsmanship. It also aimed to produce work which was uniquely Irish - in keeping with the new literary and political movements of the day. The co-operative was known as *An Túr Gloine* (The Tower of Glass), and attracted many talented artists. Two of these, Evie Hone and Harry Clarke produced works which can be seen here.

Clarke's work can be seen in St Brigid's Church,

Castleknock. The window shows three figures in brilliant medieval costume. To the left is a beautiful female St George with a sword, and below slaying a dragon. In the centre is a medieval hunter with his dog and bow. This is St Hubert, the patron saint of hunters. Below he sees the cross in the antlers of a stag, which was his conversion. To the right is a remarkable image of St Luke as an artist, with brushes and brilliantly coloured palette. Below he paints a portrait of the virgin and child. This work is strikingly original in its images and the colours are particularily brilliant. Clarke experimented in the production of new and vibrant colours for stained glass in his own workshop which he opened in 1930. The window was created in 1926 for the Brooke family.

Evie Hone's work depicts St Fiacra and can be see in St Mary's Church, Clonsilla. Fiacra was the patron saint of gardeners. Hone's work in glass was influenced by Irish and European medieval carvings, and by the great French artist George Rouault. The vibrant colours in this window are in sharp contract with the more subdued style of the day, and the figure is distinctly medieval in character. A small figure of a man digging below the saint could be from a medieval manuscript or Gothic Church.

On the social stage, the women's suffrage movement took to the streets of Dublin in June 1912, headed by the well-known suffragette Hanna Sheehy-Skeffington. One of those participating was Catherine Duffy from Blanchardstown, but originally from Athlone. Miss Duffy was arrested for, *"Wilfully damaging to the extent of £1, seventeen panes of glass"*. During the court hearing members of the Irish Catholic Women's Suffrage Association and the Church League for Women's Suffrage Societies had to be forcefully removed from the court, and were later arrested for contempt. Miss Duffy was sentenced to serve three months in Mountjoy Prison, and to pay the sum of 40s 3d. During the court case the keeper of the cells of Ship Street Barracks, where Miss Duffy was detained, reported that her behaviour was unacceptable as she caused *"major disturbances"* among the detainees. For this the Judge directed her to *"address a letter of apology"* to the keeper. On her way to prison Miss Duffy warned;

"If we have to wear out every hammer in the country smashing every pane of glass in the country, we will get our votes".

The 1913 lockout in Dublin was the most vicious labour dispute witnessed in Ireland. Each side was deeply entrenched, and involved some 20,000 workers and 300 employers. The Lockout, which began in August, warranted one entry in a local farmer's accounts journal. The farmers in the Blanchardstown area supported the Employers, and declared they would not recognise the Irish Transport and General Worker's Union after September 20th – when the corn was drawn in!

On Easter Monday morning, 1916, Dublin's racing fraternity made their way to Fairyhouse, via Castleknock and Blanchardstown, for the holiday races. The atmosphere in Dublin was relaxed – nobody in authority seemed aware that the Irish Volunteers and the Irish Citizen Army were about to launch an armed rebellion to liberate the country. Men from Abbotstown, Blanchardstown, Castleknock and Dunsink were members of the Volunteers – the First Battalion. The First Battalion of the Irish Volunteers had its origin in the Irish National Volunteers which was formed in 1913. Its members were drawn from North Dublin City. When the Volunteers split in 1914 the majority stayed with John Redmond and were known as the National Volunteers. Only a handful remained with the Irish Volunteers, but over time the numbers grew

and the First Battalion was to play a crucial role in the Easter Rising and the War of Independence.

On this particular Easter Monday a special mobilisation for the Battalion took place at Colmcille Hall, where some 300 Officers and men prepared for parade, under the command of Commandant Edward Daly. Daly told the assembled men that an Irish Republic would be declared at noon that day, and that the Battalion would shortly be in action against the British forces. They were assigned a line running from the Mendicity Institution on the south bank of the Liffey, through the Four Courts on the north bank to Cabra, where it was to contact the 5th Battalion under Thomas Ashe. Positions were immediately taken up; buildings and houses were taken over at vantage points, and barracked. Almost all of the West Dubliners were stationed at the Four Courts. This building was the repository of numerous historical documents, wills, deeds, etc. When the fighting ended great relief was experienced when it was found that the majority of these documents had not been seriously damaged. Some documents were found in the nearby streets and retained by the residents as souvenirs of the rebellion. Afterwards many of these were returned to the Records' Office. The remainder of Easter

Monday was spent strengthening the occupied positions. Out on the streets barricades were erected, often using commandeered cars and vehicles.

Within a very short time very heavy fighting had broken out all along the line. The North Staffordshire Regiment tried to cut through North King Street from Bolton Street, but were repulsed on three occasions by the Volunteers. The Volunteers were operating out of O'Kelly's Pub, Monk's Bakery and the Blanchardstown Mill shop. The Staffordshire's did eventually break through, but paid a heavy price in casualties.

The main attack was yet to come. Back in Blanchardstown an '18 pounder' battery from Athlone had detrained, and was taken to Phibsboro where it destroyed barricades on the Cabra Road and the North Circular Road. The British occupied vantage points all around the Four Courts and launched their big attack on the Thursday. The fighting was fierce, but the men of the 1st Battalion were not dislodged. The British then brought up an artillery field piece and scored four direct hits on the Four Courts. The volunteers were not prepared to merely fight defensively. They counter-attacked as required, making the British position all the more difficult. On Sunday, April 27th word came to surrender. The Dublin Brigade Review wound up its account of the rebellion thus:

"Just as no mention of the fight …. would be complete without mention of the parts played by 1st Battalion men, the fighting in the main positions occupied by the Battalion would be likewise incomplete without reference to the little band of volunteers from Castleknock and Chapelizod".

On Tuesday, May 2, three days after the rebellion ended, 289 men were deported to Stafford Detention Barracks. These included; Michael Cosgrave, Abbotstown, Andrew Dowling, Christopher Duffy, Edward Duffy, J Mooney and Patrick Mooney, Castleknock, Patrick English, Dunsink, Michael and Peadar McNulty, Blanchardstown.

Irishmen serving with the Royal Irish Regiment were among those who saw action against the rebels. Two of these were Mulhuddart men - J Keating was seriously wounded while M Carr died from wounds received.

Meantime, other men from the area were fighting on the bloody battlefields of World War I. Some, like Christopher Brennan, Blanchardstown, were professional soldiers, but most enlisted for the duration of the war. In all, 35 men from the area were killed. Most were killed in France, but five died in Turkey, two in Belgium, one held prisoner in Germany, two soldiers died at sea, and one died at the Battle of Jutland. Most were members of the Dublin Fusiliers, including Private John McAuley who died from wounds on November 11, 1918 - the day the fighting ended. Of those who died, seventeen were from Blanchardstown, thirteen from Castleknock, three from Clonsilla and two from Mulhuddart.

The attempted assassination of Lord French at the Halfway House was the most exciting event to happen in the area during the War of Independence, although local men were not involved. They were involved, however, in one of the bloodiest deeds of the war – 'Bloody Sunday', November 21, 1920. Their task was to provide cover for Michael Collin's 'Squad' which shot eleven British spies. One member of the unit was Tommy Murphy, a blacksmith from Clonsilla. He had been appointed to referee the football league match between Dublin and Tipperary at Croke Park that Sunday. He withdrew as his unit needed him, and the unfortunate man who replaced him was one of those shot dead. Some of those active in the War of Independence had also been in the Four Courts in 1916. These were Paddy Mooney,

Andrew Dowling and Michael Dowling. Other activists were Jimmy and Paddy Fernah, Michael Flanaghan, Michael Hughes, Tommy Murphy, Joe Thewles, Redcliff, Lin Dowling, Agnes Doyle, Mary Farnan, Elizabeth Kelly, Mary Lynch and Sheila Murray.

When the Civil War broke out practically everybody in the unit joined the republican side. *"Most of the unit went into the Four Courts three days before the building was shelled."* Mick Farnan was one of the youngest volunteers to join that garrison. *"He pinched a bike in Dublin, came home and changed into his best clothes and cycled back"* (Farnan Family Diary). When the fighting started his brother Paddy was seriously injured, and was eventually moved to the Mater Hospital. He had been buried under sandbags when the building was shelled by the Free State Army and suffered internal injuries. He died on July 15, 1922. Mick was captured when the Four Courts surrendered and was refused permission to attend the funeral. His father offered to go into Mountjoy Gaol as a hostage so that he might have the chance to pay his respects to his dead brother. This request was turned down. He then was given the opportunity to sign a form never to take up arms again against the State. He signed, but withdrew this when he discovered it would not take effect until after the funeral. For this he was badly beaten and dumped back into the dungeons. Paddy's remains were taken to St Brigids Church, Blanchardstown, but at first the clergy refused to receive them. A gun was put to the head of one of the priests and this brought about a change of mind!

The Civil War ended in May 1923 and in time Republican prisoners were released. The Catholic Church had supported the Free State Government and excommunicated all who took up arms against it. If these released men and women now wished to return to the fold of the Church and make their peace with God they were obliged to attend retreats to show their sincerity. The Jesuits conducted such retreats at their Rathfarnham house, and every weekend men from the Blanchardstown area headed over on the Saturday evening. The retreat lasted until Sunday evening. When the priests considered the repentants were reformed they absolved them, thus freeing them to return to normal life.

After the turmoil of the years 1916-23 the people of West Dublin returned to the task of making a living and improving their lot. One such improvement was the arrival of electricity in the

1920s. Because of its location on the Navan Road the Blanchardstown area was connected to the 10,000 Volt distribution lines, and by the early 1940s most households were electrified.

In 1935 a new Garda Station was opened in Blanchardstown. This was a source of much satisfaction for residents who now looked forward to peaceful weekends. In the absence of a Garda presence it seems pubs were showing undue flexibility at closing time. Serious drinkers from outside the area quickly learned of this situation and travelled west. When the pubs eventually closed, the revellers showed little inclination to depart. Some were moved to render a verse, or more, debate world issues with inspiring sincerity and emotion, or simply inform the world of their desire to go home, without actually doing so!

The opening of the James Connolly Memorial Hospital was the most significant event in the 1950s.Constructed on a 240 acre site (part of the Holmpatrick estate), the hospital had 540 beds and was used to treat patients suffering from the dreaded disease, Tuberculosis. The hospital was called after the Labour leader, James Connolly, on the suggestion

of Bartholomew O'Brien and his fellow Trade
Unionists.

Today the Greater Blanchardstown area is a busy,
progressive place. The population is growing, and
with it the necessary housing, services and industry.
There is even talk of building a national stadium at
Abbotstown, with the necessary infrastructure. A
returning emigrant would be quite agast at the
changes, most unrecognisable from the 1960s-70s.

One is again reminded of Shay Cullen's words:

*"Nothing much happened for one hundred years
and then everything changed overnight".*

Bibliography

Ball, F.E.	History of Co Dublin
Caproni, Vincent	A Walk Around Dublin
Carthy, James	Ireland 1851 - 1921
Cooper, Austin	A Journey from Dublin to the Shores of Lough Derg, 1741
Cullen, C. & Kelly, P	A History of St Brigid's Church, Blanchardstown 1837 - 1987
Dalton, J	History of Co Dublin
Gilbert, J. T	A Contemporary History of Affairs In Ireland, 1641 - 1652
Joyce, Weston St. J.	The Neighbourhood of Dublin

Lamplugh, G. W., Kilroe, J. R., McHenry, A., Seymour, H. J. and Wright, W. B., The Geology of the Country around Dublin

Lewis, S.	Topographical Dictionary
Longford, Elizabeth	Wellington, The Years of The Sword
McGuinness, Niamh	The Historical Geography of the Parishes of Castleknock and Clonsilla (Thesis for B.A. 1984, T.C.D.)
O'Connon Morris, W.	Ireland 1798 - 1898
O'Driscoll, James	Cnucha
Ryan, Desmond	The Rising
Sobolewski P., Langran, C.	The Blanchardstown Chronicle
Wauchopes, W.A.P.	Patrick Sarsfield

Sources

Cavendish, Catherine	The Assassination Attempt of H.L. Luttress, Earl of Carhampton,1797, Coolmine C.S. Yearbook, 1999
Gleeson, John	Blanchardstown and the Famine, Coolmine C.S. Yearbook, 2000

The Diary of Fr. Dungan

Dublin Brigade Review, 1939

Irish Times - Various Issues

1916 Rebellion Handbook

The Register of Admission and Discharge, North Dublin Poor Law Union, Vols 1-7

Ms 11657 (Walsh, R.)   National Library of Ireland

Author Acknowledgements

To my wife Muriel and children I wish to say 'Thanks' for tolerating my eccentric hobby over many years. I also wish to thank the following for the help and interest they have shown in this undertaking:

Rachel Coyle	Office of the Phoenix Park Superintendent (OPW)
Aiden Grimes	Manager, Blanchardstown Centre
Linda Halpin	Administrator, Luttrellstown Castle
Lucy Kenny	Administrator, Parslickstown House
Mrs O'Rourke	The Wren's Nest
Brian Sweeney	Assistant Estate Manager, Farmleigh (OPW)
Mr & Mrs M Traynor	The Sandpits

Dear Reader

This book is from our much complimented illustrated book series which includes:-

Strangford Shores
Dundalk & North Louth
Armagh
Belfast
Antrim, town & country
Inishowen
Heart of Down
South Armagh
East Belfast

Donegal Highlands
Drogheda & the Boyne Valley
The Mournes
Fermanagh
Omagh
South Donegal
Galway
Cookstown

Cottage Publications
15 Ballyhay Road
Donaghadee, Co. Down
N. Ireland, BT21 0NG

For the more athletically minded our illustrated walking book series includes:-

Bernard Davey's Mourne
Bernard Davey's Mourne Part 2

Tony McAuley's Glens

Also available in our 'Illustrated History & Companion' Range are:-

City of Derry
Lisburn

Holywood
Banbridge

Ballymoney

And from our Music series:-

Colum Sands, Between the Earth and the Sky

We can also supply prints, individually signed by the artist, of the paintings featured in the above titles as well as many other areas of Ireland.

For details on these superb publications and to view samples of the paintings they contain, you can visit our web site at **www.cottage-publications.com** or alternatively you can contact us as follows:-

Telephone: +44 (028) 9188 8033   Fax: +44 (028) 9188 8063